Please
Plan a Program

Please
Plan a Program

Amy Bolding

BAKER BOOK HOUSE

Grand Rapids, Michigan 49506

Copyright 1971 by
Baker Book House

ISBN: 0-8010-0527-2

Eleventh printing, April 1991

Printed in the United States of America

CONTENTS

1. The Changing Year

Leader:

As we enter a New Year today we want to think of ways we can make our lives richer and fuller for the next twelve months. Sam Walter Foss, a great poet, wrote of New Year:

> There is no bourne, no ultimate.
> The very farthest star
> But rims a sea of other stars
> Extending just as far.
> There's no beginning and no end.
> As in the ages gone,
> The greatest joy of joys shall be
> The Joy of going on.

Our speakers will tell us how they plan to go into this New Year.

First Speaker:

(Reads from the Bible) "Set your affection on things above, not on things of the earth," Colossians 3:2.

My record for the time that's past is made. I would like to change some of it but I can't. It is written forever on the pages of time. But a New Year is dawning for our lives. I plan to start by following the admonition of the Scripture just read.

People in the business world are constantly seeking to make more sales, to improve their product, to outdistance their competition. Christians should also seek to set their goals ever higher. As we start afresh we should plan to outdistance our best for our Lord. The secret of our success in the year ahead will be in the height of the goals for which we strive.

A small boy lived near a water tower. One day as he talked to a playmate he said, "This year I plan to climb to the top of the water tower."

Early one morning he went to the ladder at the foot of the tower and started climbing. As he climbed ever higher and higher he could see more and more of the things as the horizon receded. He was elated that common houses and schools looked so exciting and grand from the top of the tower.

That climb set the pattern of life for the boy. Ever as he grew he sought a higher look at problems and plans. His life was a great success.

We too will know success if we are steadfast in setting our affections on things above.

Soloist: "Another Year Is Dawning" (first stanza)

Second Speaker:

(Reads from Bible). "Many shall run to and fro and knowledge shall be increased," Daniel 12:4.

It would seem that almost a floodgate of knowledge has been opened this past year. We are no longer amazed when scientists tell us of great finds on other planets. On television we see and hear things our forefathers never dreamed existed.

As individuals we have a responsibility to increase our own knowledge in the New Year ahead of us. We are not to sit in comfort and look at what others have learned. We are to study, to go to and fro ourselves, and to help develop this wonderful world of ours by increasing our knowledge.

A woman past sixty years of age went to enroll in a college. "Why do you want to go to school where the girls wear mini skirts?" the registrar asked.

"There is so much around my world I want to know. Now is my opportunity," the woman replied.

Now is your opportunity to make knowledge increase. Find someone and impart to them your knowledge of Christ.

Soloist: "Another Year Is Dawning" (second stanza)

Third Speaker:

(Reads) "Thy shoes shall be iron and brass; and as thy days, so shall thy strength be," (Deuteronomy 33:25).

As we stand looking into a New Year it is an unknown land. We wonder what will come to our lives in the year ahead. We have been told to look above, to increase our knowledge. Now we come to the thought of bearing fruit as Christians.

When Moses was pronouncing blessings upon the children of

Israel before his death he said to Asher, "Thy shoes shall be iron and brass" — a promise that God would take care of His children as they went to conquer the land of Canaan.

Big tasks await us this year, but God still promises to give us strength as our days come and go.

A woman waiting for her husband to come back to camp after a day of hunting decided he might be lost. She took a flashlight and a lantern and started out to search for him. The man had grown confused at twilight and had started walking in circles, not realizing what he was doing. When he saw the light from his wife's lantern he called to her and they were able to get back to camp.

Many people this year will look for the light of your Christian life to guide them back to the safety of God's love.

As the woman went well prepared to search for her husband, so we must be prepared for our journey in the search for souls.

The shoes of iron and brass we have to take are the Word of God and the privilege of prayer. Much time spent with these two will give us strength for the year ahead.

Soloist: "Another Day Is Dawning" (third stanza)

Fourth Speaker:

(Reads) "Commit thy way unto the Lord; trust also in him; and he shall bring it to pass," (Psalm 37:5).

To commit our way unto the Lord means that we must trust Him. In our own strength we are helpless and afraid of the future. God has been faithful to care for us in the past and if we trust Him He will care for us in the future.

If we have trust then it follows as night the day that we will have hope. Some sorrows may come to us this year, and there may be some losses, but if we have hope in the Lord we will have strength to accept them and go on to a victorious life.

If we commit our way unto the Lord we will practice self-discipline. If we have bad habits, now is a good time to break them. The way of commitment is a narrow road and at times we may feel that it requires sacrifice, but always remember the promise, "He shall bring it to pass." So we know it is a road to victorious living.

Soloist: "Another Year Is Dawning" (fourth stanza)

Fifth Speaker:

(Reads) "Go strengthen thyself ... for at the return of the year the king of Syria will come up against thee (I Kings 20:22).

All our problems and cares do not miraculously disappear with the coming of the New Year. We can be fairly certain we will have new problems and temptations coming to us. We must strengthen ourselves in the Lord.

As we come to the close of our program we can strengthen ourselves by making some good resolutions and working to keep them.

Resolve to look to higher things by reading the Bible each day.

Resolve to learn some new thing each day and thus increase your knowledge.

Resolve to have faith that your strength will be sufficient for the task of winning someone to Christ this year.

Resolve to pray daily about your life and your goals.

Resolve to break bad habits.

(Speaker may write out the key words in each resolution on a cardboard poster for greater effectiveness.)

Leader:

We will close with a prayer.

Father, as we face this New Year may Thy grace be sufficient for our sins and shortcomings. Help us to avoid repeating the mistakes of the past. Give us strong courage and determination to face the future and live victorious lives.

2. Patriotic Program

To be effective this program needs some background props. Use a world globe on a table and hang an American flag behind. If possible, secure small flags of many countries at a book store, and stand them in pieces of styrofoam on each side of the globe.

Hymns:

"America the Beautiful"
"Battle Hymn of the Republic"
"My Country, 'Tis of Thee"

Scripture reading: Psalm 46:1-11 *(Leader and group read responsively, but all join in reading the last verse.)*

Leader:

For each of us life started with the small world of our home. As babies we knew the faces and voices of our close family. We felt secure in our familiar surroundings. When we started school, our world grew fast. We knew our school and our teachers, and our town became familiar. Then as we grew older we realized we were a part of a state. No matter what the name — Ohio, Texas, Florida — our native state became precious to us. Now we realize that we are also a part of a great nation.

What does our nation mean to you?

First Speaker:

Our nation represents to me a land of opportunity. Any boy or girl growing up in America has a chance to attend free schools. They may not always be just as that boy or girl's parents would wish but they are available. Many of our greatest leaders of the past have fought for equal opportunities for all our people.

When a person goes to apply for a job in our country he is not asked, "What class do you belong to?" He is asked, "What can you do? Are you trained?"

Ours is a land of opportunity where we make or mar our own destiny by the way we are willing to study and try.

Second Speaker:

Our nation represents to me a land where men may worship as they please without fear of persecution. I value religious freedom highly. God has given our nation the power to become great and wealthy. We have many very beautiful churches, not just in the great cities, but in the villages and around the countryside. All these churches say to us, "We believe there is a higher power and we want to worship Him."

Third Speaker:

To me our nation represents a land of free speech. We are not afraid to express our opinions and to discuss them with others. We are proud to be able to vote the way we feel is best. No one tells us how we must vote or speak.

Fourth Speaker:

Ours is a land of heroes past and present. Many people have given their lives, their time, talents and money to make our nation the great land it is today. I am proud of the heritage that is ours.

Leader:

We could go on and on telling what our nation means to us. As we come to the close of our program let us think what we can do to make our nation better. To keep our land free. Let us stand and give a salute to the flag. We will all repeat in unison:

"I pledge allegiance to the Flag of the United States of America, and to the Republic for which it stands, one Nation under God, indivisible, with liberty and justice for all."

Would you like to repeat the pledge to the Christian flag, since ours is a Christian nation?

Let us all repeat in unison:

"I pledge allegiance to the Christian Flag, and to the Saviour for whose kingdom it stands, one brotherhood, uniting all mankind, in service and love."

We will close by singing "My Country, 'Tis of Thee."

3. Christmas Program

Setting: a manger scene, several candles in candle holders. At rear of stage place a village skyline of cardboard with a light behind it. To one side, hidden by screen, arrange manger scene.

Hymn: "Silent Night, Holy Night"

Scripture Reading: Matthew 1:18-25a and Luke 2:8-20a. *(Use the version, Good News for Modern Man)*

(Leader lights the tallest candle on the table. Places it near the manger scene.)

Leader:

When Christ was born over two thousand years ago, some people called him Emanuel. *Emanuel* means "God is with us." We want God to be with us tonight as we celebrate the birthday of Christ.

(As the speaker tells the story of Christ's birth let children of appropriate sizes, be angels, shepherds, wise men. They can walk across a dimly lighted stage like a tape rolling over and over as the story is told.)

Leader:

This was the way that Jesus Christ was born. Mary his mother was engaged to Joseph, but before they were married she found out that she was going to have a baby by the Holy Spirit. *(A large angel walks slowly across the stage.)*

Her husband Joseph was a man who always did what was right *(Joseph walks across with bowed head)* but he did not want to disgrace Mary publicly, so he made plans to divorce her secretly. While he was thinking about all this, an angel of the Lord appeared to him in a dream *(Joseph lies down on a bench at back of stage, the large angel comes back and hovers near him)* and said: Joseph, descendant of David, do not be afraid to take Mary to be your wife. For the Holy Spirit is the father of her child. *(Mary walks*

slowly across the stage from one side to the other.) She will give
birth to a son and you will name him Jesus — for he will save his
people from their sins. Now all this happened in order to make
come true what the Lord had said through the prophet: *(A prophet
walks across and goes off stage.)* "The virgin will become pregnant
and give birth to a son, and he will be called Emanuel" (which
means "God is with us").

(The angel leaves the stage.) So when Joseph woke up he did
what the angel of the Lord had told him to do and married Mary.
(Joseph leaves the stage; then he and Mary, side by side, walk across.)
But he had no sexual relations with her before she gave birth to
her son. And Joseph named him Jesus.

Hymn:

> O holy child of Bethlehem! Descend to us, we pray,
> Cast out our sin, and enter in; be born in us
>   to day,
> We hear the Christmas angels, the great glad
>   tidings tell,
> O come to us, Abide with us; Our Lord,
>   Emmanuel.

Leader (lights another candle and sets it near the manger scene.)
(Prayer)

Oh, God of love, be with us here tonight as we seek to worship
and honor thy son Jesus Christ. Amen.

There were some shepherds in that part of the country who
were spending the night in the fields, taking care of their flocks.
*(A number of shepherds walk on one side of the stage. As the
reading continues angels come to the other side of stage. If a spot-
light is available shine it first on the shepherds, then on the angels.)*

The Lord's angel appeared to them, and the Lord's glory shone
over them. They were terribly afraid, but the angel said to them:
"Don't be afraid! For I am here with good news for you, which
will bring great joy to all the people. This very night in David's
town a Savior was born — Christ the Lord! This is what will prove
it to you: you will find a baby wrapped in cloths and lying in a
manger. . . ."

When the angels went away from them back into heaven, the
shepherds said one to another, "Let us go to Bethlehem and see

this thing that has happened, that the Lord has told us." *(Shepherds walk across stage and move screen to expose manger scene.)* So they hurried off and found Mary and Joseph, and saw the baby lying in the manger. When the shepherds saw him they told them what the angel had said about this child. All who heard it were filled with wonder at what the shepherds told them. Mary remembered all these things, and thought deeply about them. The shepherds went back, singing praises to God for all they had heard and seen. *Shepherds sing:* "Joy to the world!"

(Leader lights the third candle.)

Leader: Three lighted candles could mean many things. I believe that on the night of Christ's birth they could have represented the presence of God, the presence of the Holy Spirit, the presence of the Holy Child.

Today we might think of the three candles as representing God in our Church, Christ's love in our home, the Holy Spirit at work in the world.

(Final scene: All members of cast march on stage and group around Mary, Joseph and Babe in manger, as the music of "Silent Night" is being played. When all are in place the group sings "Silent Night.")

Leader:

Thank you, dear Heavenly Father, that you loved the world enough to send Your son to die for our sins. Amen.

4. Easter Program

Hymn: "Up from the Grave He Arose"

Scripture: I Corinthians 15:20, "But now hath Christ been raised from the dead, the first-fruits of them that are asleep."

Leader:

Eternal life is the thought on our minds this Easter Sunday. Each Easter we think anew of the victory over death and the grave. Our faith is renewed and strengthened as we review our hope in Christ.

We may walk boldly in the garden of our world today. We can shout the joy we feel that we are His and He is ours.

First Speaker:

Resurrection is the fulfillment of Scripture.

Resurrection is a Christian certainty. "I shall see him but not now" (Numbers 24:17), was spoken concerning the coming of Christ by a prophet in a trance.

"If a man die shall he live again?" (Job 14:14).

Men of all ages have asked this question. Some have believed and prepared for the dawn of a new day after death.

In Revelation 20:13, we read that in the judgment day even the sea will give up its dead.

Philippians 3:10 mentions the power of His resurrection. Many people looking out over their yards and gardens this Easter morning saw bits of green stems and leaves breaking through the ground, heralding the flowers that would soon be blooming, resurrected from their long sleep.

> God gave unto us a beautiful lily
> With a fragrance, rich and rare,
> Bless'd it with His love divine
> As it blossoms, sweet and fair.
> He chose a bit of purest white
> And a tint of sunset glow,

Gently molded them into a flower,
And sent it to us below.

A word need not be ever spoken
By that lily, pure and fair,
For a Saviour's message will be revealed
As its fragrance fills the air.
There in a lily's purest heart
Dwells the sweetest blessing ever born;
A message sent from the Christ above
To us on Easter morn.

— P. F. Freeman

Second Speaker:

The resurrection is a commission to serve.

Christ gave this commission after He arose from the grave and before He ascended into heaven. He commissioned His followers to "Go ye into all the world and preach the gospel."

Forget not the glorious Easter when Christ arose. Look with sorrow at the Cross of Calvary and remember the price of redemption. It was to the cross Christ went to pay for our sins. It is to the cross of repentance we must go if we would be saved to serve.

Only twelve apostles and a few other followers were commissioned to witness against a pagan world; to bring in a Kingdom they could not see. The task seemed impossible.

Today as we think of the multitudes who reject all we consider holy, our task seems too great. But remember the disciples went out and won the people in great numbers because they had seen the risen Lord. Philippians 3:10 reads, "That I may know him and the power of his resurrection."

If we have really seen the risen Lord we will want to make Him Lord of our lives. If He is Lord of all, then we must give Him all by serving. How can we serve? He gave us the way, "Go ye,... preach."

Third Speaker:

The resurrection is an answer to doubt.

We go about showing such doubtful hearts. I wonder if instead we should not shout over and over, "Christ arose, Christ arose!"

Whenever doubt is mentioned, we automatically think of

Thomas. Yet Thomas did believe when he looked upon the risen Lord, and we have such wonderful opportunity to look upon the miracles God has performed in this world; we have the living love of Christ in our hearts. Why then do we doubt?

We often deny that we doubt, yet we live from day to day as if we had never heard of a risen Lord.

When doubt assails us we have but to look at God's world to see how nature constantly comes again to life in the spring; we have but to look at the changed lives of people who were lost in the depths of sin who, when they met the risen Lord, arose to walk in newness of life.

> Some sweet morn a day will open,
>   Never more to close in night;
> We shall hail the early token
>   Of its everlasting light.

> On that bright and blissful morn,
>   Pilgrims rest, their journey o'er:
> Hunger, thirst, and death, and sorrow,
>   We shall know and fear no more.
>   — Unknown

Fourth Speaker:

There is victory in the resurrection.

Everyone likes to be on the winning team. Jesus kept assuring His followers they were on a winning team; but on the day they saw their leader die, they could think only of defeat.

Three days later, however, they tasted victory. Christ arose! During the forty days He spent with those who loved Him, He made some promises.

One I especially like is Matthew 26:64, "Henceforth ye shall see the Son of man sitting at the right hand of power and coming on the clouds of heaven."

As children we often liked to lie on the grass and look up into the beautiful sky, picturing Christ coming down to call us to heaven.

For over two thousand years Christians have been singing songs of victory. Christ's resurrection inspired a small handful of poor fishermen to start a movement that has been felt around the world. He has freed us from the grave. He has bought us with a price.

We are the redeemed of the Lord.

Hymn: "Christ the Lord Is Risen Today"

Leader:

Is there someone here who would like to testify of the hope that is within her/his heart because Christ is alive forever more?

Dear Father, as we join the mighty victory song of the Christian people today, may we never forget our own commission. Inspire us to go and tell the story, bringing the hope of salvation to the lost of the earth. Give us power from the One who conquered death. In Christ's name we pray. Amen.

5. State of the Church Program

This should be a program given at a banquet or meeting of all the church at the beginning of the new year's work. The object is to stress the good points, acknowledge the weaknesses of the past and put forth goals for the future.

The printed program might be similar to the following:

S .... Serve with music. Songs by congregation.
T .... The Word of God. Bible reading.
A .... Appreciation and recognition of any visitors.
T .... The reports of nominating and other committees.
E .... Entrusted with responsibilities.

O .... On the mission front.
F .... Filled with the Holy Spirit. A prayer.

C .... Call for reports from heads of departments.
H .... Heaven will come down. Goals for next year.
U .... Uniform work for the improvement of church.
R .... Regular attendance, visitation, giving.
C .... Calling for your best. A message by the pastor.
H .... Happiness is success. Closing song and prayer.

WE DARE NOT FAIL

Leader: "Declare his glory among the nations, his marvelous works among all the people" (Psalm 96:3).

Hymns:
"Jesus Calls Us"
"Stand Up for Jesus."
"There's a New Day Dawning"

Scripture: John 21:16; Galatians 6:2

Leader:

We are met here for our annual State of the Church Banquet. Do we have visitors in our group? We welcome you here and hope you will receive an inspiration from the reports and messages to-night.

We will at this time have a report from our committee on committees.

First Speaker (Chairman of Committee on Committees):

(It is well to have mimeographed sheets of all the committees to pass out. Your church may not have all the committees listed. Call on the ones you do have.)

As I read the name of the committees will the members of that committee please stand?

Baptism, Benevolence, Church Historian, Counting of Money, Education, Enlistment, Evangelism, Flowers, Retreat and Camp, Greeters at Doors, Insurance, Kitchen and Food, Library, Lord's Supper, Missions, New Member Welcoming, Offering for Morning, Offering for Evening, Planning for Calendar, Recreation, Trustees, Ushers, Nominating.

Thank all of you for taking places of responsibility. Will each chairman try to meet with your committee soon and make your plans for the future months?

Second Speaker:

As a worker in this church organization we are entrusted with the responsibilities of helping our fellow members grow and develop. I think I can best tell you how I feel by reading this poem:

> Our Master toiled, a carpenter
>   Of busy Galilee;
> He knew the weight of ardent tasks
>   And ofttimes, wearily
> He sought, apart, in earnest prayer
> For strength, beneath His load of care.
>
> He took a manly share of work,
>   No thoughtless shirker, He.
> From dawn to dusk, before His bench,
>   He labored faithfully.
> He felt just pride in work well done
> And found rest sweet, at setting sun.

His Father worked, and He rejoiced
        That honest toil was His —
To whom was given grace to know
        Divinest mysteries;
And shall not we find toiling good
Who serve in labor's brotherhood?
                        — Thomas Curtis Clark

(Used by permission of Harper and Row Publishers.)

Third Speaker: (Regarding work on the mission front. *Give a report on gifts to missions during the past year. Give excerpts from any letters the church may have received from missionaries. Reads Psalm 96:3)*

Fourth Speaker: Pray for the growth of missionary zeal in the church.

Leader: (Call on the superintendents of the various departments for reports on highlights of the past year.)

Fifth Speaker: (Educational director or Sunday school superintendent gives goals and highlights of plans for the future.)

Sixth Speaker: Reports on uniform work for the improvement of church. Urges each worker to be faithful, reads the following poem:)

The fight is pretty stiff, my boy,
        I'd call it rather tough,
And all along the routes are wrecks
        Of those who tried to bluff —
They could not back their lines of talk,
        To meet the final test,
You've got to have the goods, my boy,
        And that's no idle jest.

                                    — Unknown

Seventh Speaker: (Reports on the average Sunday school attendance for the past year.)

Pastor's message: "Calling for Your Best."

Leader: (Announces closing and leads in prayer.)

6. Man's Greatest Power

Hymn: "I Choose Jesus"

Scripture: Deuteronomy 30:19

Leader:

It seems only human for people frequently to say, "If I could choose, I would be thus and so."

> If I could be the sun for just one day,
> I'd open every bud that bloomed my way.
> I'd scatter every shadow, every shade
> That fell across my path, and make them fade.
> I'd warm the hearts of men and make them glad;
> I'd make a world of joy where all was sad.
> I'd draw the perfume from a rose, and hold
> It for a soul with mocking world grown cold.
> I'd shine through every cloud and make for you
> A golden lining in a sky of blue.
> And when night came, I'd quietly go my way —
> If I could be the sun for just one day.
>
> — Christel Hastings

Do you think having the ability to choose makes man greater than other creatures created by God?

First Speaker:

In Genesis 1:26, we read, "And God said, Let us make man in our image, after our likeness."

In making man in His image, God gave man the power to choose. Man may choose between good and evil, he may choose between working hard or being lazy, he may choose between being good humored or bad tempered. This list of choices is endless.

Other creatures have very little choice in life; they are ruled and dominated by man.

Yes, I would say having the power to choose makes man the greatest of God's creations.

Man may decide to take huge machinery and build a dam that will destroy natural beauty, or will cover hundreds of acres of land with water. The choice is man's to make. God has given him dominion over the earth so he chooses what he will do with the things upon the earth.

Because of the ability to choose man is constantly being challenged to accomplish greater things.

Second Speaker:

There are, however, some things we cannot choose. We cannot choose our parents, the country in which we are born, nor the color of our skin. We come into the world helpless, yet I believe there is a Heavenly Father who chooses these things for us. He has a plan and a purpose for our lives, yet He gives us a choice in working out that plan and purpose.

Help in making choices in life is available to us as Christians. If we are faithful in reading our Bible, the choice between right and wrong is not hard for us to know.

There are, of course, other choices. We must often choose between certain jobs. Youth must choose which courses to take in school, what they want most to accomplish in life.

Christians have the greatest help in the world — the help of prayer. We can in prayer pour out our problems to God. He will send the Holy Spirit to guide us in the right direction. The solution to any problem begins with choice. We may choose to ignore all help and advice, to make our own mistakes. We may choose to talk with our parents or our pastor, we may choose to pray quietly and alone and work out our problem, but we are free to choose how we will face each problem.

Third Speaker:

I wish to present a slightly different slant from that presented by the other two speakers. I believe our choice of companions is one of the most important and life shaping of any.

There was once a boy who was compelled to move frequently because his father was a military man. His mother taught her son one rule to follow in choosing friends. She said, "You will be judged by the friends you choose so be sure they are clean, honest, and intelligent."

Another woman made this rule for her daughters when they started dating. Never accept a date with a boy you would not want to marry. Other girls often made fun of her daughters because their mother was so strict, but this mother knew that girls who choose with care the boys they date will make good marriages and will not suffer the sorrow of a broken home.

The responsibility of choosing our companions is one of the greatest responsibilities we will be called upon to meet; yet the right choices promise great rewards and often result in lifelong friendships.

Fifth Speaker:

I would like to mention the choice of our attitudes. We choose to be happy or sad, we choose to be humorous or solemn. God said, "Choose life, that you ... may live." Some people choose just to exist, others choose to work and develop their minds and abilities to the greatest extent.

Two teen-age children were placed in a home for orphans. The boy determined to get all the education he could and make something of himself. The girl determined to find a way to get out of the home so she could be her own boss. The boy studied hard. Evenings, in the impersonal study room of the home, he worked and dreamed of the time when he would be a man and know how to work and succeed.

The sister ran away and married the week after she graduated from high school. She thought she was choosing a wonderful way to freedom. Her life became one of hardship and trouble.

The boy was often lonely and at times very tired but he kept on until he finished college. He had a good life and found that his choice of taking advantage of his opportunity to get an education paid well in the long run.

I have noticed some people choose to be cross early in the morning. Couldn't they just as well choose to be happy that they are alive and face a new day?

Our choice of being happy or sad affects others.

Leader: Do you think we have a right to make a choice if it hurts others?

Sixth Speaker:

When we are faced with a choice that might hurt others we have a responsibility to study the issue carefully. A lawmaker often chooses to vote in the way he feels will gain him the most votes. A minister sometimes chooses to preach sermons he feels will make him popular. Yet we have a responsibility in all choices to ask God's will and choose the way He would approve. God will give us grace and sustain us if we make the choices He would have us make.

Some people try to avoid making a choice. They ask someone else to take the responsibility. Those who do this are giving up a gift from God, the gift of choosing.

If a lawmaker chooses to vote in favor of liquor and gambling, he hurts others. Children will go hungry and homes will be broken because of the choice he made.

If a minister chooses to ignore sin and wrongdoing in his sermons, his choice is wrong. People may go in the wrong direction because he failed to warn them.

The power to choose is God's great gift to man. The fact that we abuse that choice and fail often is our own fault.

Leader: Rescue missions all over our land are filled with people who made wrong choices. We must determine to meet our responsibilities by making the right choices.

Closing prayer

7. Useful Bridges

Hymn: "Jesus Saves" or "The Haven of Rest"

Scripture: Ephesians 2:8, 9

This program can be given by one person. If one person takes all the parts, he should secure some building blocks or tinker toys and build a bridge across two boxes as he talks.

Leader:

As we were growing up we often played "London Bridge Is Falling Down." This "bridge" was formed by two children holding hands high, to make an arch under which the other children passed.

Today we want to think about useful bridges we find as we travel through life.

First Speaker:

Because the foundation of the old London Bridge started sinking into the clay of the river banks, London authorities decided to dismantle the bridge and build a new one at a cost of $7,000,000. That was a very expensive bridge.

Yet we have all heard of a bridge that cost much more. Jesus Christ became the bridge whereby we might span the chasm between earth and heaven. This bridge cost our Saviour suffering, persecution, ridicule, death. When He hung on the cross in the most terrible of mortal agony, at the last He cried, "It is finished!"

Did He mean His life was finished? I do not think so, for He had said He would rise again in three days. He was thinking of the bridge whereby man could cross from death into life eternal. He had finished paying the price for our sins.

> The hands of Christ
> Seem very frail
> For they were broken
> By a nail.

But only they
    Reach heaven at last
Whom these frail, broken
    Hands hold fast.
       — John Moreland

Used by permission of *Decision Magazine*

Second Speaker:

No other bridge is necessary. John 14:6 reads, "Jesus saith unto him, I am the way, the truth, and the life: no man cometh unto the Father, but by me."

A certain truck driver refused all his life to attend church. He denied the existence of God and in many ways was very wicked. One day as he was going down the highway with a huge load of merchandise he saw a car ahead of him go out of control and run into a river.

He stopped his truck and jumped into the water and managed to save the two children in the car. He went back to try to save the driver but his clothes were so water soaked and he was so exhausted, that he drowned in the attempt.

The man's wife said to her friends, "God will take him to heaven because he gave his life for others."

We know, however, that even if he had saved a hundred lives he could not cross that bridge built by our Lord in any other way than by believing on the Lord Jesus Christ. There is no other way.

Acts 4:12 says, "Neither is there salvation in any other; for there is none other name under heaven, given among men, whereby we must be saved."

Third Speaker:

This is not a toll bridge. There are still a few bridges where people must stop and pay toll before crossing. Many years ago there was such a bridge between the towns of Purcell and Lexington, Oklahoma. The river there was shallow at certain times of the year. At such times many farmers would refuse to pay the toll, and would drive their teams across the shallow stream to the opposite shore. Sometimes they would get into quicksand. If they were lucky help would arrive and they would be pulled out, but some wagons were sucked down into the sand. Yet they took this chance to save just a few cents.

Jesus paid the price to bridge between the chasm of death and judgment. The bridge is accessible to all without payment of toll.

A parent does not ask a child to pay each day for food and care, it is given freely with love. So Christ has paid for our salvation, He asks only that we believe. In Isaiah 55:1 we read, "Ho, everyone that thirsteth, come ye to the waters, and he that hath no money; come ye, buy, and eat; ..."

Many people have gone before us over this bridge, many will come after us.

Fourth Speaker:

Will this bridge fall down?

Some years ago as people were passing over a bridge on their way home from work, a span of the bridge gave way. Many people plunged through the gap and were killed. The bridge literally "fell down." It was the only bridge crossing the river that divided a busy city from the large residential area where the workers lived.

We step on the bridge to Heaven by faith. We live by faith in our Lord, and well we may for this bridge will never fall down.

The nails in this bridge were stained with the blood shed on the Cross of Calvary. Our bridge is spiritual and wonderful. We can go about singing praises and shouting, "Glory to God in the Highest."

> O what a wonder that Jesus found me,
> Out in the darkness, no light could I see;
> O what a wonder, He put His great arm under,
> And wonder of wonders, He saved even me.
>   — Ralph Schurman

Fifth Speaker:

Do we have a duty concerning this bridge?

One day Jane and Tom were alone at home. The doorbell rang and a package was delivered, a package from their Aunt Maggie. The children opened the package. Inside they found a beautiful box of candy. Each child took one piece. The candy was so good they took another piece. Then they talked about how much fun it would be to hide the candy and eat some each day after school before their mother came home from work.

In just a few days the two had eaten all the candy. They put the box in the trash and said not a word to the rest of the family.

Our actions are far worse than those of these selfish children when we fail to go out and tell the lost world about the bridge built by Jesus' love. Jesus commissioned us to go and tell the world. We have no excuse for not telling others.

The more of Christ's love we give away the more there is filling our own hearts.

Leader: So we have a bridge that is given us freely, it is available to all, it is safe, and it lasts eternally. We too can build bridges daily, bridges of love, kindness, sharing, hope, good news. Let us be about the business of bridge building.

(Closing prayer)

Father take from our hearts all selfishness. Make us reflect the great love manifested by our Saviour on the cross. We pray in Christ's name. Amen.

8. Let There Be Light

Hymn: "Send the Light"

Scripture: Genesis 1:3, "And God said, let there be light: and there was light."

Leader:

Coming up to my own door the other evening, I suddenly thought of lights — all kinds of lights. A light was burning on the porch, to light the way to the door. A very small light shone through the button on the doorbell, to point out to visitors where they might ring for attention. Going into the hallway, I glanced up at the overhead chandelier. In the living room I saw a table lamp; over the piano hung a chain lamp. In the other rooms I found a variety of lamps and lights. There was even a small light above an oil painting to enhance its beauty. There was a high intensity, infrared lamp for health purposes.

How like God's world! He has put many people here to give forth the light of His love. Some shed very meager light, while others are very bright; but all have a purpose and are useful if turned on.

First Speaker:

There is a blackout in parts of the world.

"I am come a light into the world, that whosoever believeth on me should not abide in darkness" (John 12:46).

In 1965 there was a great blackout in eight states on the Eastern seaboard. Many people were caught in the tall buildings of New York City and had to spend the night where they were or grope their way down many flights of stairs by the light of cigarette lighters or matches. Pilots, ready to land, saw all the lights suddenly go out. Thirty million people were in darkness.

On that terrible night in the Northeast people reacted in many different ways. Some thought a fuse had blown in their own homes, some blamed the power companies. All asked, "What happened?" Some took advantage of the situation — people paid as high as seven dollars for a candle. Flashlights were sold at even higher prices. Taxi drivers charged enormous prices to take people home.

Wherever people looked that night they found not only that electric lights had gone out; machines run by electricity were useless, too. When there is no light our world finds itself in a terrible condition.

There will come a time in this world when the power of Satan will be no more.

Second Speaker:

"Yet a little while is the light with you. Walk while ye have the light, lest darkness come upon you: for he that walketh in darkness knoweth not whither he goeth" (John 12:35).

Five boys were in a dormitory room. One of them was twenty years old, he had been in college two years, yet to him the world looked dark. His parents had separated and his father was planning to marry again.

"Why should we study and try to be good?" he asked the others, and he gave to each a cigarette — Marijuana! The police had been watching the dormitory and that night they raided the rooms. The five boys were put in jail.

Why are so many people lost in the darkness of despair today? People have more light on more subjects than ever in history. Where once we had to grope our way to the center of a room and pull a chain for light, now we can walk through a beam of light and a door opens automatically.

Darkness represents sin. People living in sin are in darkness as far as their souls are concerned. We who have the light of God's love cannot even fathom the blackness and despair that makes a youth throw away his changes in life for a thrill, or a few moments lost in a haze of dope or a drug.

Third Speaker:

Lucky, indeed, on the night of the great Northeastern blackout were those people who had some type of reserve power. The telephone company was able to function, some hospitals had reserve systems, most radio companies could operate because they had reserve power plants.

As Christians we have reserve power for any emergency. If we are living for God and trying to send His light into the world we hold a candle in the darkness. In New York City, that fateful night in 1965, many people learned the art of sharing. Many people with cars stopped and asked strangers to ride, many who had candles shared with friends.

People all over our country have personal blackouts. Some have family problems, some financial, some problems of drink. There are many broken hearts because of death or tragedy. You have a candle of hope in your heart; share it with those in need.

Psalm 23:4 offers hope to those who walk through the valley of the shadow of death. Is it too hard to quote or read to others?

A boy in an institution for correction was planning to take his own life. He felt his parents hated him, his friends would look down on him when he was released. The day he planned to carry out his suicide, he was called to the visitors' room.

A man who had once been the boy's school teacher had stopped as he was passing through town and made the extra effort to visit the boy.

As they visited the teacher tried in every way to help the boy see that when he was released he must try very hard to succeed in school and in life. That candle of encouragement and hope kept the boy from taking his own life. In time he did become a success in life, all because one person cared enough to give him a glimmer of light in a dark world.

Fourth Speaker:

Time does not permit us to read all of II Peter 2:4-22. Verse 17 reads: "These are wells without water, clouds that are carried with a tempest; to whom the mist of darkness is reserved forever."

If we do not want to live in darkness forever we must accept the light. We must give the light to others.

Hell is black! There is a fire there that will burn forever, but it will offer no light, no hope. If we turn away from the salvation offered by Christ we turn only to darkness.

But we do not have to be cast into outer darkness. David said, "The Lord my God will enlighten my darkness" (Psalm 18:28).

Can't you imagine how wonderful the daylight looked the morning after the blackout? Many people who had taken the sun for granted before appreciated that sunrise. We may not take God's love and light of salvation for granted.

Our salvation was paid for at great price by one who cared for us. Can we do less than accept it and be thankful?

A mother and father sat by the bedside of a very ill child all night. They sat in a very dim light hoping the child would relax and sleep. As the early morning light started coming in the windows the little one looked up and said to her parents: "Now God is awake to see about me, why don't you go to bed?"

We do not have to see the light in God's heavens to know He is awake to see about us. We only have to accept the light of His love.

Leader: As a closing prayer I would like for us to reach out to the ones sitting near us and hold hands as we sing, "All to Jesus I Surrender."

9. The Bible

Hymns: "Break Thou the Bread of Life," or "Holy Bible, Book Divine."

Scripture: Isaiah 40:8, "The grass withereth, the flower fadeth: but the word of our God shall stand for ever."

Leader:

The Bible

The charter of all true liberty.
The forerunner of civilization.
The molder of institutions and
    governments.
The fashioner of law.
The secret of national progress.
The guide of history.
The ornament and mainspring of
    literature.
The friend of science.
The inspiration of philosophies.
The textbook of ethics.
The light of intellect.
The answer to the deepest human
    heart hungerings.
The soul of all strong heart life.
The illuminator of darkness.
The foe of superstition.
The enemy of oppression.
The uprooter of sin.
The regulator of all high and
    worthy standards.
The comfort of the sorrowing.
The strength in weakness.
The pathway in perplexity.
The escape from temptation.
The steadfast in the day of power.
The embodiment of all lofty ideals.

> The begetter of life.
> The promise of the future.
> The star of death's night.
> The revealer of God.
> The guide and hope and
>   inspiration of man.
>   — William F. Anderson

First Speaker:

The Bible is made up of many books. There are thirty-nine books in the Old Testament, twenty-seven in the New Testament, making a total of sixty-six books in all.

The Bible contains books of history, poetry, prophecy, and letters.

The Bible was not written all in one period of time. Over a period of about fifteen hundred years many writers wrote the different books. Some of the writers of Old Testament books we know best were: Moses, Solomon, David, and Isaiah. In the New Testament we find the Gospels written by Matthew, Mark, Luke, John. We find letters written by Paul. Many other inspired writers we will not have time to mention.

The Bible or parts of it have been translated into almost one thousand languages and dialects.

Many missionaries and translators at great personal sacrifice and hardship have gone to live in foreign lands to learn languages in order to translate the Word of God for the natives of those lands.

During the Dark Ages people sought to destroy the Bible. God preserved copies so that it would not be lost to man. God takes care of His own and He has taken care of this wonderful book for us.

Second Speaker:

Is the Bible the Word of God?

The Bible seems to be the Word of God. Yet is that enough proof? The history of the Book and its preservation through the ages is good proof. The contents of the Book are so ancient yet so modern, someone who could see down through the ages must have inspired the writing. Someone with power to fit the whole together must have hovered near as it was written. So it seems to be the Word of God.

The Bible itself claims to be the Word of God. Matthew 24:35

reads, "Heaven and earth shall pass away, but my words shall not pass away."

I Peter 1:25 says, "But the word of the Lord endureth forever."

In Exodus we have the story of God giving Moses instructions to write the law.

Communications from God were given in different ways. Some men had "visions," some had "dreams," God spoke to Moses, "mouth" to "mouth."

The disciples saw and heard much of what they wrote. The writers of the New Testament referred to the Old Testament.

Christ used the Old Testament in His ministry. He referred to it in His messages, He read from it in the synagogue. He seems to have memorized much of the Old Testament. He believed the Bible to be powerful and true.

Third Speaker:

An American lady traveling in Switzerland about one hundred years ago found the following poem written on the walls of the inn. She translated it and brought it back to America.

Old Testament

In Genesis the world was made by God's creative hand;
In Exodus the Hebrews marched to gain the promised land;
Leviticus contains the Law — holy, and just, and good;
Numbers records the tribes enrolled, all sons of Abraham's blood;
Moses, in Deuteronomy, recounts God's mighty deeds;
Brave Joshua into Canaan's land the host of Israel leads;
In Judges their rebellion oft provokes the Lord to smite;
But Ruth records the faith of one well pleasing in His sight;

In First and Second Samuel of Jesse's son we read;
Ten tribes in First and Second Kings revolted from his seed;

In First and Second Chronicles see Judah captive made;
But Ezra leads a remnant back by princely Cyrus' aid;
The city walls of Zion Nehemiah builds again;
While Esther saves her people from plots of wicked men;
In Job we read how faith will live beneath affliction's rod,
And David's Psalms are precious songs to every child of God;
The Proverbs like a goodly string of choicest pearls appear;
Ecclesiastes teaches man how vain are all things here;
The mystic Song of Solomon exalts sweet Sharon's Rose;

While Christ the Savior and the King, the "rapt Isaiah" shows;
The warning Jeremiah apostate Israel scorns;
His plaintive Lamentations their awful downfall mourns;
Ezekiel tells in wondrous words of dazzling mysteries;
While kings and empires yet to come Daniel in visions sees;
Of judgment and mercy Hosea loves to tell;
Joel describes the blessed days when God with man shall dwell;
Among Tekoa's herdsmen Amos received his call;
While Obadiah prophesies of Edom's fall;
Jonah enshrines a wondrous type of Christ our risen Lord;
Micah pronounces Judah lost — lost, but again restored;
Nahum declares on Nineveh just judgment shall be poured;
A view of Chaldea's coming doom Habakkuk's visions give;
Next Zephaniah warns the Jews to turn, repent, and live;
Haggai wrote to those who saw the temple built again,
And Zechariah prophesies of Christ's triumphant reign;
Malachi was the last who touched the high prophetic chord;
Its final notes sublimely show the coming of the Lord.

New Testament

Matthew and Mark and Luke and John the Holy Gospels wrote;
Describing how the Saviour died; His life and all He taught;
Acts proves how God the apostles owned with signs in every place;
St. Paul in Romans teaches us how man is saved by grace;
The apostle in Corinthians instructs, exhorts, reproves;
Galatians shows that faith in Christ alone the Father loves;
Ephesians and Philippians tell what Christians ought to be;
Colossians bids us live for God and for eternity;

In Thessalonians we are taught the Lord will come from heaven;
In Timothy and Titus a bishop's rule is given;
Philemon marks a Christian's love which only Christians know;
Hebrews reveals the Gospel prefigured by the law;
James teaches without holiness faith is but vain and dead;
St. Peter points the narrow way in which the saints are led;
John in his three Epistles, on love delights to dwell;
St. Jude gives awful warnings of judgment, wrath and hell;
The Revelation prophesies of that tremendous day
When Christ, and Christ alone, will be the trembling sinner's stay.

Leader:

We must not let so great a treasure as our Holy Bible go neglected. We should read and study some from its pages each day.

In this land of light and freedom,
    Where the Gospel's often heard,
Men will close their eyes in darkness,
    And despise God's Holy Word:
While the heathen now in darkness,
    Blindly groping in the night,
Hearing once the sacred story, gladly
    Turn unto the light.

(Closing Prayer)

Father, make us aware of the truths found in Thy Word. Make us aware of our responsibility to spread the gospel. Give us a determination to read and study more the great truths now, should the day come when we are not so blessed with freedom to do so. Thank You for the great men who have preserved and translated Thy Word for us.

(Closing Hymn) "Wonderful Words of Life"

10. Vital Witnessing

Hymns:

"Throw Out the Lifeline"
"Bring Them In"
"Send the Light"

Scripture: Luke 5:10.

Leader:

We have not been converted just for our own ease and pleasure. True, people who belong to and attend church are usually better adjusted and happier than others; but there is a purpose for our lives.

What do you feel is the main purpose in the life of a Christian?

First Speaker:

Luke 5:10 tells us Jesus promised His disciples He would make them fishers of men. I think we are to seek for lost men to bring them into the Kingdom. We too are to be fishers of men.

In years past women often knew many home remedies for common ailments. They would go to a friend's home in time of sickness and help by nursing the sick and using their remedies. They were anxious to tell what they thought would cure a disease.

If we have a cure for sin and unhappiness in this world, we should be glad to tell our remedy to our friends and neighbors.

I would say the main purpose in the life of a Christian is to become a fisher of men.

Second Speaker:

Not all people have the ability to win the lost. I feel there is a definite gift from God to those who have such an ability. Sometimes we are afraid of making a mistake. The person we wish to win may live a very moral life.

Leader:

Could it be that we sometimes fail to believe a person is lost?

Third Speaker:

That reminds me of a story I heard about a Mr. Rowe who lived in a community of Christian people. He often did nice things for them. He kept his house and yard very clean. He owed no one. Each year when revival time came around a few friends would ask him to join their church. He always said a polite, No.

When Mr. Rowe was past middle age a young man came to the community for evangelistic services. He went to the home of Mr. Rowe. He read the verse, Romans 3:23, "For all have sinned . . ."

"Now, Mr. Rowe, you are a lost man if you have not trusted Jesus as your Saviour." He went on to explain the plan of salvation. Mr. Rowe was saved and joined the church. On the night he joined he asked to say a few words.

"I knew you people had something I did not have. I tried to live as near perfect as I could but I felt a lack. This young man boldly told me I was not perfect and showed me the way."

We are often just too timid to tell a man he is a sinner. We should pray for power and courage, then use what God gives us.

The disciples were untrained men but with the power of Christ in their hearts they were successful as fishers of men.

Fourth Speaker:

We should make some definite plans about how we will go about witnessing. In our Bible we might place a list of the unsaved people we know. Then we can proceed.

We should pray for the ones on our list every day and ask God to give us a way to reach them.

I believe it would be best to take one name from the list and start cultivating that person as a close friend. Win his confidence. Tell him your opinions about Christ but be patient to listen to his own viewpoint of life.

At an opportune time in your friendship tell your friend about the time Christ came into your own life and the change it has made.

Ask outright if he would like to become a Christian.

Have Scripture passages marked and ready to read at the right moment.

Be on close terms with the pastor and take your friend to counsel with him.

When one has been won, write the date of victory by his name in your Bible and start on the next name God leads you to.

Leader:

In closing I would like to observe, this is one task we learn by practice and prayer.

(Closing Prayer)

11. God's Luggage Shop

Hymn: "Make Me a Blessing"

Scripture: Matthew 25:18-29

Leader:

A large family was preparing for a vacation trip. The mother gave each child a piece of luggage and told them to pack what they needed to take on the trip. The pieces of luggage did not all match — they had been accumulated over the years and were all sizes and colors.

When all the suitcases were packed and the day of departure came, the father of the family fitted all the luggage into the trunk of the family automobile.

Does a story such as this remind you of anything in our daily lives?

First Speaker:

I am thinking we are all children of the Heavenly Father and He has given each of us a piece of luggage to pack for our journey through life.

We might think of our talents as our luggage. Some have bright shining talents, others only small abilities. The time will never come when every person is born with exactly the same amount of talent and ability.

Second Speaker:

You are right about the difference in our talents but I believe each person has the responsibility to use what abilities he has. There is a boy in one of our Western cities who sings in the choir at each morning worship service. Now, there are eighty other young people in that same choir, all just as faithful as Teddy. Teddy just happened to get a very faulty piece of luggage when the bodies were handed out. He is paralyzed from the waist down and has to swing along on crutches. He is often a burden to the other choir members as they march into the choir loft. As Teddy stands leaning on the rail in front of him with crutches under his arm many people are blessed by his sheer determination to keep trying. He is packing his small piece of luggage with all the joy and blessing he can be to others.

Third Speaker:

I would like to hear Teddy sing. There is in our own vicinity a fine looking young man who was given the very latest in style and color as far as fancy luggage is concerned. He is handsome, fairly well-to-do, and has a pleasing personality. I am afraid when he arrives at the end of the journey and opens his luggage he will find only emptiness. He is not packing any service or goodness to take on his journey through life. He thinks only of pleasure and fun. He considers trying to be of service to the world as being a "square."

If only we could realize we will not be given a chance at a second trip!

Fourth Speaker:

Once there was a family living in California. Although the parents had grown up in New York State, the children had never been out of the state of California. The parents saved their money, planning to take the children to New York.

The mother went to the grocery store and secured a number of nice clean boxes. She labeled each box with the name of a day, then she packed what she thought the family would need that day in that box. All the boxes fit nicely together in the car. There was very little confusion on the trip because they just unpacked one box a day.

If we as human beings could only learn to fit together in God's world there would be so much more accomplished.

Fifth Speaker:

Sometimes people just refuse to make the most of life because they feel they were short-changed when the luggage was given out. Two girls graduated from high school. One worked hard to get a scholarship for college; the other girl complained because her parents were not wealthy so she would have to get a job and forget college. Years later the girl who refused to work hard for a scholarship was jealous of the one who had worked and succeeded.

It isn't the size of the luggage that counts or its good looks, it is how we use each piece.

Leader:

Looking around our group I see all kinds of talents. Some are good speakers, some are good musicians, some are good at cooking, some at organizing. The important thing is to take the luggage God has given you and make the most of your journey through life.

Sixth Speaker:

To me it seems we have left out something important!

A small boy was told to pack a bag for a trip to his grandmother's. When he arrived at the grandparents' home his bag contained a ball and bat, a handful of string, a funny book, a small telescope, some colored rocks, and a frog in a small box. There was nothing he could wear or use.

We need to examine our lives and see if we have packed a lot of jealousy, envy, greed, lust, evil, pleasure, and useless things. If we have, now is the time to determine to throw them out and re-pack.

Leader:

As we have our closing prayer let us pray that each person here will use the luggage God has given him to the very best of his ability, disposing of all worthless and useless things.

12. Christian Tests

Hymn: "Give of Your Best to the Master"

Scripture: Matthew 7:16-20

Leader:

This is a day of testing. We find children in school taking tests. We find men competing for jobs taking tests. In all of life there are tests, and by the tests people are judged and classed. Do you think there are tests for Christian people, too?

First Speaker:

I always think of the attendance test. There are some Christians who will be found in their church for every service, regardless of the weather.

Many attend only on special days, when they feel it may add to their prestige. Many people attend services only when their favorite minister is in charge. I believe a real Christian will attend as often as he possibly can, regardless of who is the leader.

A new minister was sent to a church. He happened to be nice looking and unmarried. The attendance among the young ladies tripled almost overnight. When after a few months he picked out one woman for his wife, the attendance among the young women dropped back to normal. The incentive seemed to be gone. I believe a real Christian attends church because he loves the Lord and His work.

Leader:

That reminds me of a little story I read about two church members who were out on a lake fishing.

"This is prayer meeting night," one remarked.

"Well I couldn't have gone anyway — my wife is sick."

"I think the weather is too bad to get out," the friend replied; and they went right on fishing not even noticing the misting rain.

Second Speaker:

The test I like to use on a Christian is what I call the *work test*. Every person has some time off from the work they must do in order to make a living. Some people spend a part of their free time working for their church. The men in a small church painted the inside of the building. The women, not to be outdone, brought coffee and cookies to serve the workers.

People can't always be painting or cleaning on a church building but they can be willing to help when needed. Working together at a common task makes people better friends.

Third Speaker:

At the risk of being thought mercenary I would like to mention the *pocket book test*. A man in a certain small church wanted to control every penny that was spent. He often resisted progress and the church grew very slowly. A new pastor with progressive ideas came to this church. At the first business meeting he conducted, Mr. Brown successfully vetoed every project the new pastor suggested. The pastor was very disappointed but not defeated. He did some checking and observed the church members carefully.

At the next business meeting the pastor presented the same plans. Mr. Brown made the same objections.

"I have noticed that Mr. Brown never contributes to the church," the pastor said. "Why should he tell the rest of you how to spend your money?"

The people began to follow the pastor and the church grew and prospered. Mr. Brown could not stand the pocket book test.

Fourth Speaker:

We should think again about our Scripture for the day. The person who never wins another to Christ does not meet my test for a Christian. If we really trust and love Christ as our Saviour we will want to tell others about Him. We will find ways to let people know what a wonderful life the Christian life is. In other words we might say there is a *fruit test* for every Christian.

Leader:

I would like to read a poem before our closing prayer

Definition of a Christian

He has a mind and he knows it;
He has a will and shows it;
He sees his way, and goes it;
He draws a line, and toes it ;
He has a charge and takes it;
A friendly hand and shakes it;
A rule and never breaks it;
If there's no time, he makes it.
He loves the truth, stands by it.
Nor ever tries to shy it,
Whoever may deny it, or openly defy it.
He hears a lie and slays it;
And, as I've heard him praise it,
He knows the game and plays it,
He sees the path Christ trod,
And grips the hand of God.

— Unknown

(Closing prayer)

13. Your Church

Hymn: "The Church's One Foundation"

Scripture: Matthew 16:18

Leader:

We often speak of "The Church," "Your Church," "Our Church," "His Church," "The Early Church." In this program we want to take a good look at the church founded by Christ and what it means today.

First Speaker:

Often when we speak of "The Church" we mean no more than a certain building located in a certain place. Church buildings are important because they represent the place we go to be closer to God and to worship Him. In Ephesians 2:20-21 the spiritual church is compared to a building. Christ is called "the chief corner stone."

People love their church buildings and often make great sacrifices to pay for them. Some modern thinkers feel that in the next decade church buildings will not be needed and people will meet in smaller groups in homes and in parks.

A Baptist minister in Houston, Texas, is experimenting with this type of organization at the present time. Only time will tell about such things as this. The church building offers many advantages: adequate space for teaching, a place where all races and social levels may meet and feel welcome. A church building offers a place where we can show our love for God in a material way. We are told in the New Testament to bring our offerings into the storehouse.

We must conclude that the church building has its place of service just as important as that of the Temple in Bible times.

Second Speaker:

Let us turn our attention to the church as a group of organized believers. In Romans 12:5 we read, "So we, being many, are one body in Christ, and every one members one of another."

In Matthew 16:18 we read that the gates of Hell shall not prevail against the church.

In the early days of our country people of like faith came in groups to settle the new land. They were often cruel and unjust to those who did not worship in the same manner.

Through all the changes and upheavals of time the church Christ started lives on. An old hymn reads:

> O where are kings and empires
> > now,
> Of old that went and came?
> But, Lord, thy Church is praying
> > yet,
> A thousand years the same.

Soldiers in the World Wars have visited many beautiful cathedrals and churches, yet they worshiped in tents and in open fields under the direction of a chaplain. They could not establish an organized group and keep it intact for many years. I believe they were serving God just as much as the people in the big church buildings. Most of them were a part of some church organization back in the States. Many Christians took time to write regularly to those members of their churches who were far away.

Third Speaker:

There are so many different denominations and groups that we should carefully choose the one to which we give our loyalty. Many people automatically join the same church their parents belong to. Some drift from one group to another as their mood changes.

I don't believe Christ came to establish a denomination but to start the Kingdom of Heaven. The groups of organized believers help promote His kingdom.

We should study the New Testament and make a list of the rules and suggestions laid down for church membership. Then we should study the doctrines and beliefs of the church we want to join and see if we agree with its teaching.

Most denominations and churches have three things in common:

1. The principle of love — love that finds its roots in God; love that sacrifices for a cause; love that knows no barriers.

2. Freedom — a soul freedom that recognizes only the Lordship of Jesus Christ. We were slaves to sin, but since giving our hearts to Christ we know freedom. We find we have a freedom of the will, given us when God created man.

3. Cooperation — the church seeks to bring in the Kingdom by cooperating together in love and freedom. Working together, a number of people can build schools, hospitals, churches, where one working alone could not accomplish these goals.

The church is the only institution Christ started during His earthly ministry. It is a divine institution.

Fourth Speaker:

Most of the members of most churches have accepted Christ as Saviour. They have no authority to make commandments so they seek to obey the commandments given in the New Testament. We believe the commandments and rules of governing a church come from God. By faith we seek to follow His teachings.

What purpose did Jesus have in establishing a church? Christ saves individuals, not groups, yet He had a purpose for the church as an organization.

Christ gave mutual responsibilities to the church members as a group. He is the Head of the church and gave Himself for it.

Christ established two ordinances while here on earth: the ordinance of Baptism, showing the death, burial and resurrection of the sinner; and the Lord's Supper, an ordinance to help us remember our Lord and the price He paid for our salvation.

Both these ordinances are to be administered by the church. If the church should disappear, the ordinances also would be lost in the way Christ meant for them to be administered.

The church will never outgrow the Great Commission until Christ comes again. The ends of the earth have not yet been reached with the gospel.

Fifth Speaker:

We have said very little about the officers in the church. In I Timothy 3:2, twelve bishops and deacons are mentioned. Both officers are to be filled with a certain type man.

The bishop, or pastor, is a shepherd of the flock.

The deacon is the helper in the management of the affairs of the church.

Leader:

> God of the living church, we plead,
> Bestow Thy mighty power,
> Thy loving presence, Lord, we need,
> To save us in this hour.
>   — A. H. Ackley

14. Let's Face Ourselves

Hymn: "Oh Master, Let Me Walk with Thee"

Scripture: Romans 8:5, 9, 14

Leader:

In this age of hurry, we need at times to stop and face ourselves. We, like a merchant, must take an inventory. Have we shown a profit or a loss in the past? As you listen to the speakers apply what they say to your own life and decide your own answer.

First Speaker:

First we will think about our own personal problems. People can be of very little use to the world if they are overpowered by their personal problems.

To live is to have personal problems, how we meet and solve them makes the difference.

A very common personal problem is that of disliking some person where you work. Maybe you feel that person gets advantages others should have. Maybe you are just jealous because he seems to have more friends in the office than you have. Whatever the reason, to dislike some one you work with in any situation is a serious problem.

There is a way to solve the problem. First you need to pray for yourself and for your enemy. Pray as unselfishly as possible. Try to see his side of the picture.

In a certain chain store the assistant manager felt animosity toward the head of the meat department. The man often came to work late. The assistant manager asked the manager to fire him but the manager refused. One day when some reports were due the head of the meat department was absent. The manager asked the assistant to go to a certain address to get the reports filled out.

When his enemy opened the door and invited him in, the assistant manager saw a different person. He was wearing an apron and held a crippled child in his arms.

"You see, my wife had polio a few years ago before the baby was born, and he was injured at birth. Most of the time she can care for him from her wheel chair, but today she is ill and can't get up."

The assistant manager went away thanking God for his blessings and determining to help his former enemy.

If our lives are filled with the Holy Spirit we will seek to understand the people we dislike. Understanding usually makes us at least more tolerant.

Second Speaker:

We face ourselves in the gifts we give. Our attitude toward giving tells much about us. Many of us want the world to think we are generous and helpful. When we really examine our hearts we may find we are grasping and selfish.

A very selfish greedy, grasping woman one day came face to face with tragedy. Her only son was seriously injured in a wreck. As she tried to pray and ask God to spare his life, all her shortcomings seemed to stand out in her mind. At last in desperation she confessed her sins and humbly asked God to save the life of her child. We might say she caught a glimpse of Jesus. Her son did live and her life changed. She spent her time helping others.

If we face ourselves in the light of Christ's sinless life we will want to give more money, love and time to His service. We can only change our habits and activities when we really catch a glimpse of Jesus.

There is no way we can outgive our Lord. He will always take our gifts and multiply them many times over.

Remember the little lad who gladly gave his loaves and fishes to Jesus. Did he know what the Master wanted with them? I don't think so. He gave because the Master needed them. Then it was that Jesus multiplied the food in order that all might be fed. No doubt the little lad went home with a full heart, and perhaps a full basket of food.

Third Speaker:

James says in his letter, "Ye have not because ye ask not."

Let us face ourselves concerning our faith.

We often hear the expression, "I have faith to believe." Is that true? There was once a prayer meeting in Texas. The people met to pray for rain. Crops were ruined and cattle would soon die for lack of water. A large group came to the church to pray. Only one little old lady brought her umbrella. Who had faith to believe God would send the rain?

The Scriptures say, "Whatsoever ye shall ask in my name, believing, ye shall receive."

We must face ourselves and see if we believe. Many people succeed in life just because they have faith to believe they will succeed. If we have faith in ourselves, we have only partly won the battle of life. If we have complete faith in God we have won completely. If God sees fit not to let some of our ambitions and dreams come true, if our faith and trust are in Him, we accept His will and are happy.

Fourth Speaker:

We face ourselves in Bible study. We would not think of sending our soldiers into battle without weapons. Yet we often go out into the world to face the darts of Satan without having read or studied our Bible. The Bible is the sword of the Lord and we have it at our disposal if we only put forth the effort to use it.

From Genesis to Revelation the Bible is the greatest book one can read and study. There are love stories, war strategies, law, history, poetry and philosophy. With such a book available why should we want to read any other?

The Bible

Read it to be wise,
Believe it to be safe,
Practice it to be holy,
Memorize it to grow.

It involves the highest responsibility,
    It will reward the greatest labor,
It will condemn all who trifle
    With its sacred contents.
                              — Unknown

Fifth Speaker:

We face ourselves as we give. There is always some need to be met in our world. If not in our city, then in the next one. How we respond to needs tells us the state of our hearts.

An elderly couple visited an orphanage one afternoon. The longing of the children for just a loving touch from a human hand, impressed them. After they returned home they talked about the needs of the children. They were too old to take children into their home, but a plan came to them after much prayer. Each visiting day they would take enough quarters to give one to each child. For a hundred children it did not add up to much for the wealthy couple. The children were so happy to have that little bit for their very own.

We are plainly taught in the Bible what God expects us to give back to His work. Are we trying to get by with doing less?

Some are glad to give money but never give of themselves. They are too busy to attend services or make a visit. Let us face ourselves — do we want to share with the needy world?

Leader:

We have faced ourselves in a number of ways. Have we gained new visions of what we can do? Have we had new impressions of the needs of our lives for more spiritual growth?

(Closing prayer)

15. Building Personality

Hymn: "Just As I Am"

Scripture: Luke 3:9

Leader:

We want to think about each person being a personality apart from all other people, and about how that personality develops.

You Are Only You

There's a certain job God's given you
  That no other soul on earth can do.
If you don't do it the best you can
  It won't be done by another man.

He's given you powers with which to work
  And don't you dare His job to shirk.
He depends upon you to do your part
  For He's put His love into your heart.

We sometimes think we're of no use
  To His great work — That's no excuse
For not doing the job we should.
  And we could do it if we would.

So you get busy with the job,
  Or from your heart it's going to rob
You of God's powers that He will give
  To bless your life as long as you live.

— Unknown

First Speaker:

Environment is a great factor in the building of a person's personality. If a child grows up in a home where there is lots of love and tolerance, his own personality will reflect this. If he never knows quiet and peace, only hears criticism and bickering, he will grow up with the same attitude.

A young woman found she was pregnant just a few days before

her husband was shipped overseas in the Korean war. She was very bitter for a few moments, then she thought of her child. "I will think only sweet and happy thoughts while I am bringing this baby into the world," she promised herself.

As the child grew people remarked about what a good, sweet, helpful girl she was. Her mother always said in her heart, "She has been reared in that type home."

We would not expect people who had known life only in the highest social circles to step into the rugged existence of the slums, and know how to survive.

Because I believe strongly environment develops a person's personality, I think it is important for us to invite and enlist people to attend our church. There they are exposed to the power of God's love as shown by the people who follow Him.

Second Speaker:

One of the greatest factors in personality development is the friends a person associates with. This probably overlaps the environment angle. Yet people are free to choose who will be their friends wherever they live. There are "heels" in high society, middle class society, and in the lowest class known. People who have high ideals and who strive to be better are also found in every class. We choose the type we will make our best friends.

Man is naturally in need of companionship. We are made in the image of God. He said He made man to have fellowship with Him, so He must like companionship also. Good friends of high ideals help us develop into the kind of person we want to be.

King was a boy who longed to be a minister. His father said he must be a lawyer. He felt lonely and miserable. At college his best friend was a boy who was planning to enter divinity school. As they talked and planned together his friend gave him some advice.

"Go on through college, keep your father happy by getting a law degree, as we write and visit I will teach you all I learn in the divinity school."

The young men wrote often. The law school and the divinity school seemed very similar in many ways. They were both learning to work with people.

Just a week after being admitted to the bar, the young lawyer

was called home to attend his father's funeral. He was grateful
he had pleased his father by taking the law course. As soon as the
estate was settled he started to preach. With the aid of his good
friend he was able to secure a church. His friend helped him
develop patience and tolerance during the time he needed it most.
God was really at work in his life for as time went on he became
president of a religious school and his law training was very useful.

The wrong friend would have advised him as a college boy to
break his father's heart and have his own way.

Third Speaker:

A pleasing personality is made up and developed from many different things. In the business world the young person who develops
a habit of being grateful for favors is likely to succeed. Thank you,
is a simple phrase, yet it develops a pleasing personality. Someone
has said, "The most important thing a mother can teach her young
child is to say, 'Thank you,' for everything done for him." We just
naturally like to be kind or helpful to those who appreciate our help.

Developing an attitude of gratitude helps develop a pleasing personality. Boys like to take out girls who show appreciation for the
good times they have.

The Christian who develops an attitude and habit of being
grateful to God for His blessings has a happy, pleasing personality.

Fourth Speaker:

Personality is developed by our sense of purpose, or our lack of
purpose in life. The person with a goal in view works in many
ways to press toward that goal. People in free societies develop happier personalities because they can have a purpose and work to
achieve it. Happiness is trying to attain our purpose in life.

Along the same thought we might say, to develop a good personality we must have a desire for that accomplishment. Some
people do not try to improve their ways. Often a person will be
rude or too outspoken. They will excuse themselves by saying,
"That is just my way."

We should try to change our ways into those of a gentle person.
The people we like best are those who try to be a blessing to the
world. To be that type of person one must desire to constantly
improve and to develop better traits.

High moral principles come from noble aspirations. As we practice gratitude, kind words, good companions, faith in our fellow man, we grow into a better personality.

Fifth Speaker:

You May Count That Day
If you sit down at set of sun
And count the acts that you have done
And counting find
One self-denying deed, one word
That eased the heart of him who heard,
One glance most kind
That fell like sunshine where it went —
Then you may count that day well spent.

But if, through all the livelong day
You've cheered no heart, by yea or nay,
If, through it all
You've nothing done that you can trace
That brought the sunshine to one face,
No act most small
That helped some soul and nothing cost —
Then count that day as worse than lost.
— George Eliot

Leader:

Let us close with a prayer.

Lord, help us to realize we are the ones who must shape our personalities. Give us courage to try to be better and more useful each day. Amen.

16. A Living Sacrifice

Aim: To develop right attitudes concerning one's divine gift from God, our bodies.

Hymn: "Give of Your Best to the Master"

Scripture: Romans 12:1

Leader:

We will have a panel discussion. We will ask questions concerning our bodies and the right way to treat them. There is much discussion today concerning the use of drugs, the prevalence of heart trouble and other diseases.

A Pastor:

I will try to discuss the question, "What is meant by a living sacrifice?"

You have heard it said at times it is easier to die than to live with the trouble one faces. God wanted us to live, and to live in service for Him. James Russell Lowell said:

> Words, money, all things else are comparatively easy to give away; but when a man makes a gift of his daily life and practice, it is plain that the truth, whatever it may be, has taken possession of him.

Whatever your daily tasks may be, live for God while working to accomplish them.

A Physician:

Do many young people today harm their health by trying to live like the "gang"?

Many high school and college students start on the downward road to poor health and broken lives just because they were chicken to say No when offered drugs, or strong drink. It would be well to memorize our Scripture for this program and remember it when tempted. In one town of one hundred fifty thousand, a survey was made in the high school. Ninety per cent of the students said they had been offered drugs by friends. A lower per cent said they had experimented with drugs.

Can we present our bodies wholly acceptable to God if we damage our brain or our hearts by indulging in drug usage?

Drugs are not the only harmful practices available to young people today. There is much danger to health for any one who engages in illicit sex affairs. Venereal diseases are common among certain groups of young people.

The body is a very wonderful and complex gift from God. We should strive in every way to take good care of it.

A Nurse:

I will try to give a few thoughts on physical fitness. There seems to be a great revival of interest in all kinds of physical fitness programs. People can start almost any kind of course on health. Health related businesses are booming. Older people seem to be the most interested. Could it be they now see the results of some of their follies in youth?

Youth today often neglects proper exercise. It is not popular to walk when one has a car handy. It is easier to sit in a comfortable chair and look at television than to play an active game in the fresh air.

We should seek physical strength and health so that we can serve God to the best of our abilities.

A Teacher:

What type of pupil is best adjusted in the school room?

I might start by saying we have some pupils who go to the snack bar or vending machines at noon. They drink a coke and eat a candy bar — that is their lunch. That type pupil is often absent with colds or other health problems. We find that the pupils who eat a balanced diet at lunch are more alert and less susceptible to diseases.

The body is a very delicate machine and it must have proper food and exercise. For this reason most schools have a physical education program as well as reading, writing, and arithmetic.

The human mind and body can be trained and taught more

than any other being God created. Teachers are powerless when pupils abuse and destroy the mind and body.

Policeman or *Lawyer:*

God asks for a living sacrifice. That means a person who will live for Him daily. He does not ask for cold, formal rituals. Many of the youth who come to the attention of the law, do so because they were not kept busy. They grew bored and restless. A chance to get in trouble seems like just a chance for a thrill or a little excitement.

Our churches must offer more and more activities for the youth. Maybe the church didn't have a ball team when grandma was young, is it a sin to have one now? Often a ball team or a mission project will keep young folk off the street and occupied. Paul said he could be all things in order to win some.

When you see a young person in trouble ask yourself, did I try hard enough to help that one?

Leader:

Paul asks for a living sacrifice. We might say he asks for our love to be laid on the altar.

At a summer camp a small child was drowning in the deep water into which another child had pushed her. A lifeguard quickly jumped in and rescued her. As he held her in his arms later the little one patted his face and said, "I haven't any money but I will give you all my love."

The lifeguard said that was the greatest thanks he had ever received from a rescued person.

God asks for our love. Other things will inevitably follow.

Let us pray:

May we today present our whole being a living sacrifice on Thy altar, dear God. Amen.

17. Individual Responsibility

Hymn: "Is Your All on the Altar?"

Scripture: Romans 14:12

Leader:

In recent years we have seen our nation develop into a country where people blame others for the difficulties they face. The blacks blame the whites, the young blame the old, the rich blame the poor, and vice versa. Few stop to take a long look at their own responsibilities. Romans 14:12 says, "So then every one of us shall give account of himself to God."

There are seven fields in which we need to examine our responsibilities: our actions, our time, our words, our ways, our works, our money, our life as a whole.

First Speaker:

Our actions. I Samuel 2:3, ". . . and by Him actions are weighed."

We cannot excuse ourselves when we go with the crowd in wrongdoing by saying, "Everybody does it." God weighs our individual actions and we will each be punished or rewarded for these individual actions.

Someone described the human life as a song that God has already written. It is our responsibility to read the music and sing the song. It is so sad that so many fail to seek God's will and consequently never find the truly great music God plans for them.

Sam had been very naughty so the teacher had to take him out of the classroom and administer punishment. When she asked him why he was so naughty he sobbed and said, "My mommie wouldn't listen to me when I told her what I wanted in my lunch."

Was Sam at fault or was his mother?

We do not have that same excuse for our wrong doing. Our Heavenly Father is ready to listen at any time day or night.

Second Speaker:

Our Time. Matthew 20:6, 7. "...Why stand ye here all the day idle?"

A man was very busy getting ahead in his job. His wife often asked him to attend church services with her but he always replied, "Later, when I have succeeded."

At last there came a day when he was rich and successful. Then his reply to his wife's pleas was, "I wouldn't know what to do, I am too old."

We have no time to stand idle in the work of bringing in the Kingdom. Today is the day to work. We are never too old to repent and go to work in God's service.

Each person is given twenty-four hours in a day, we are responsible for the way we use those hours. It is nice to have some time for resting. It is needful to have some time to make a living. It is rewarding to take some time to serve the Lord.

Third Speaker:

Our Words. Matthew 19:36. "But I say unto you, that every idle word that men shall speak, they shall give account thereof in the day of judgment."

If we could remember this verse when we are having an argument, or indulging in gossip, or angry with some person, we would stop before committing such sins.

A small child was told by his older brothers to stay in the house while they went to a vacant lot to play ball. He felt hurt and slighted. Noticing a puzzle on the table, he picked up the box and ran outside. One end of the box had a hole in it and the pieces began to fall out as the little boy ran across the vacant lot toward his brothers. By the time they were able to get the box from him most of the puzzle pieces were lost. The child tried to go back and pick them up but he could never find all of them.

Idle or angry words can never be brought back and closed up in a box, once they have been spoken. We may think the words are forgotten or forgiven, but Scripture says we will have to give an account in the day of judgment.

Fourth Speaker:

Our Ways. Psalm 119:168. "For all my ways are before thee."

At times we have all heard someone say, "Well that is just my way."

Is the above statement an excuse for people being unkind or rude? At times we defend a friend who has been unkind by saying, "That is just her way."

If we have ways that are not kind and sweet we should seek to improve them. There is a guide for this improvement. People buy books on health, on diet, on psychology, on many types of improvement of the body and mind. We have the greatest book in the world on the improvement of our ways. The Bible. You cannot read a chapter a day in the Bible without finding yourself just practicing better ways; without assuming a better attitude toward your family and friends.

Psalm 1:6 tells us God knows our ways. This should inspire us to attempt to make them ways to be proud of.

Fifth Speaker:

Our Works. Isaiah 66:18. "For I know their works and their thoughts."

Tom was a farm boy. When his father went to town and left him to work in the field, he would run to the woodlot to play. When his father came home he would be very disappointed that the weeds had not been cut from the field.

We often act like Tom. Because our Saviour has gone to heaven for awhile, we run and play in the world and neglect to bring in the Kingdom.

In I Corinthians 3:13 we read, "Every man's work shall be made manifest; for the day shall declare it, because it shall be revealed by fire."

Sixth Speaker:

Our Money. We are responsible for the material possessions God has given us. He provides a plan that is fair to all. He asks for one-tenth of all we make. If we make a large amount our tenth is large.

Kraft, the great cheese man, tells how he had a wagon loaded with cheese on a hot day. He just could not seem to sell any and in the heat his product would soon spoil. He stopped the wagon on a side street and talked to God. He promised God if He would help him sell the cheese he would give a tenth to God's work. From that day on his cheese began to sell and he developed the great Kraft industries. He not only paid a tenth to God's work but was able as time went on to give much more than a tenth.

We should not pay a tithe to God just for what we will receive in return, but for the love we have in our hearts. Mark 12:41 reads, "And Jesus sat over against the treasury, and beheld how the people cast money into the treasury."

What does He see today as the offering is made in our churches?

> One-tenth of ripened grain,
>   One-tenth of tree and vine,
> One-tenth of all the yield
>   From ten-tenths rain and shine.
>   — Unknown

Seventh Speakers

Our Life. Romans 14:8: "Whether we live therefore, or die, we are the Lord's."

The following poem by an unknown writer in a church paper expresses our thoughts of the responsibility of a person as a whole.

> It's not the words you sing to me
> Or the tune that's set there-to,
> It is the life I want to see
> And to know the things you do.
>
> It's not the range of voice you have
> To warble high or low,
> It's how you live the song you sing
> That I would like to know.
>
> It's not the gestures that you make
> When to the throng you sing,
> It is the man behind the song
> That I would tribute bring.
>
> For if the man who sings to me
> Has failed to live his song,
> He fails to touch this heart of mine
> Because his heart is wrong.

Leader:

As we remember the different phases of life for which we are

responsible let us close with a silent prayer that we will become
more conscious of our individual needs.

(Pause) . . . Amen.

18. Higher Ground

Hymns:
"Higher Ground"
"O Master, Let Me Walk with Thee"

Scripture: Philippians 3:13-14

Leader:

Many Christians fail to reach great heights as workers in Christ's kingdom because they fail to set high goals. We would think in this program how we can press toward the prize.

First Speaker:

In 1938 at Dartmouth College a young man by the name of Glenn Cunningham reached the top as a runner in track events. You would have to hear the story of Glenn as a boy to realize what a great accomplishment this was.

To start a fire in the stove, Glenn poured on the embers what he thought was kerosene. However the can had been filled with gasoline and in the ensuing explosion his brother was killed and Glenn was badly burned.

The doctor said Glenn would never walk again. Glenn, however, determined he would walk. His parents massaged his legs when they began to heal and after many months he could walk a little. He determined to run. And run he did until in college he broke records as a runner.

Second Speaker:

I don't think people should stop when they think they have reached the top. Glenn Cunningham received a Doctor's degree from New York University and became a teacher. Always he felt God had spared his life for some purpose. He did not realize what that purpose was until he became a wealthy man owning a large ranch. He began to take unfortunate boys and girls to live on the ranch. He and his wife loved the young people they took into their home. As time went on they helped over 8,000 boys and girls. I would say Dr. Glenn Cunningham pressed toward the mark.

Third Speaker:

Perhaps at times we fail to aspire to higher levels. We fail to set goals and then strive to reach them. Life is a struggle. We never stand still. If we are not going upward, we are going backward. It is up to us to set our goal and press forward.

Paul said, "I have fought a good fight."

Some people talk a great deal about trying to reach higher levels but they never seem to do so.

> The fight is pretty stiff, my boy,
>   I'd call it rather tough,
> And all along the routes are wrecks
>   Of those who tried to bluff —
>
> They could not back their lines of talk,
>   To meet the final test,
> You've got to have the goods, my boy,
>   And that's no idle jest.

Fourth Speaker:

One of the best ways to reach any goal is to prepare. We live in a day and age of education and special training. It is important to get all the training and education possible. One man said he wanted an education because it was a big stick with which to fight the world.

There are other things needed besides preparation. One is faith — faith in God and faith in oneself. Faith in God will give a person courage when things look dark. Faith in oneself will give one strength to keep trying. We never know when the next step will put us on the victors' side, we must just keep going.

Fifth Speaker:

Another thing we have not mentioned is that of goals. A robber might have a goal of robbing a bank, even might carry out his plan, but that does not make him a better man or the world a better place.

As a Christian we should want to make the world a better place because we lived in it.

Sometimes people are afraid to set goals because they fear failure. Henry Ford once said: "Failure is only the opportunity more intelligently to begin again."

How much richer our world is because Henry Ford was not afraid to keep trying.

Leader:

As we go home let each one look up at the sky and resolve to try for higher things, earthly and heavenly.

Let us close with this prayer:

Guide us in our daily ambitions and plans, we ask in the name of Christ our Lord. Amen.

19. Christ above Things

Hymn: "Hallelujah! What a Saviour"

Scripture: "Wherefore God also hath highly exalted him, and given him a name which is above every name," Philippians 2:9.

Leader stands at front while the speakers and chorus march in from the back singing, "Stand Up, Stand Up, for Jesus." Each member could carry a lighted candle. The house lights could be turned off for the march and when all are in place on the stage the candles may be blown out and lights turned on.

Leader:

As we march through this life in the service of our King, we want to be sure we place Christ above earthly things.

A soldier during World War II was determined he would not go to the front lines. When the order came for his unit to move to the battle area he sat in the back of the truck. As they bumped along over a mountain road he managed to slip off the truck and hide in the trees. When the troops arrived at their camping spot, the soldier was missed. His platoon leader sent two men back down the road to look after him. They found his body torn to bits by a bomb the enemy had dropped behind the lines.

We often destroy ourselves because we put our comfort ahead of our service to our Christ.

First Speaker:

Wanted: Men!

Men of spirit, men of will,
   Men of muscle, brain and power,
Fit to cope with anything —
   These are wanted every hour.

Not the weak and whining drones
   Who all troubles magnify;
Not the watchword of "I can't,"
   But the nobler one, "I'll try."

Do whate'er you have to do
    With true and earnest zeal;
Bend your sinews to the task,
    Put your shoulder to the wheel.

Though your duty may be hard,
    Look not on it as an ill;
If it be an honest task,
    Do it with an honest will.

In the workshop, on the farm,
    At the desk, where'er you be,
From our future efforts, men,
    Comes a nation's destiny.

— Unknown

Second Speaker:

Is Christ First?

There are many things to put first in our world today. If we are industrious we may work long hours to succeed in our business or job. We often feel we are neglecting our family in this effort to make money.

A wealthy family living in a beautiful home near a lake, came home one night from the city to find their home and everything in it burned to the ground. Friends living around the lake had gathered to be present when the family returned. Knowing how proud the wife had been of some of the beautiful pieces of furniture they expected to hear loud lamentations.

As the car stopped and the man, wife, and three children stepped out to view the ruins, the crowd gathered around were astounded at the words of the wife.

"Thank you, dear God," she said, as tears streamed from her eyes. "You were so wonderful to let us have our children with us."

She never ceased to be grateful that God had spared her most precious possessions. Her family!

Do we get caught up in a race for more things and forget to put Christ first?

An old minister used to quote Matthew 6:33, as follows: "But seek ye first the kingdom of God, and his righteousness; and all these things (all that you need) shall be added unto you."

Third Speaker:

Working for Christ.

We are to put Christ above all things even if we are tired; even if we are poor, or ill. If we put Christ truly first in our lives we will have a peace that cannot be bought with money.

> A matchless honor, all unsought,
> High privilege, surpassing thought
> That Thou shouldest call us, Lord, to be
> Linked in fellowship with Thee!
> To carry out Thy wondrous plan,
> To hear Thy messages to man;
> "In trust," with Christ's own word of grace
> To every soul of human race.
>
> — Unknown

Leader lights each candle again as the organist or pianist plays, "We're Marching to Zion." As each candle is lighted its bearer marches down the aisle, the leader only remaining on stage.

Leader:

(Closing prayer) Help us to resolve tonight to put Christ above the acquisition of earthly things. Amen.

20. Memory Time

(A program to be given in a convalescent home for aged people.)

Leader:

As we sing or quote Scripture or poetry, you are invited to sing or recite with us. We would like for you to do so.
Hymn: "What a Friend We Have in Jesus"

First Speaker:

I will read some favorite passages from the Bible. (*Read* John 14:1-3, Psalm 23, John 3:16.)
Hymn: "Amazing Grace"

Second Speaker:

Have you noticed lately how beautiful the sunset hours of the day are? You are in the sunset days of life and I hope each day is precious and beautiful to you. At times you grow lonely for loved ones and friends who are far away from you. There is a way you can feel closer to them and be a blessing to them. You can pray for your dear ones as you sit in your room. You can name them over one by one and ask our Heavenly Father to bless each one as they need blessing at the moment.

Once there was a young minister who became very discouraged. He felt he was a failure because very few new people were being won in his church.

On Sunday things took a strange turn. At the close of the service a number of people asked to join the church. There was much rejoicing among the congregation.

That afternoon the minister went to visit a member who was crippled and could only get about in a wheel chair. As he told her of the great service that morning she was happy.

"I knew you would have a great service," she told him. "Last night I could not sleep so I prayed for·you and for the people, I felt God heard my prayer and would answer."

You see even in the sunset of life you can bring good and blessings to others by praying.

Leader:

We will have a prayer at this time.

Third Speaker:

Some of the greatest stories in the Bible are about people who were old in years but young in spirit.

There was Moses. He was a great leader up until the time of his death at age 120. Then the one who followed Moses as leader was Joshua. Joshua lived to be 85. Some of you are older than that. God lets people live as long as He has a purpose and use for their lives. You may not know that purpose, but God knows. Accept each day as a gift from God and try to enjoy that day by making someone happier. Just a kind word to the nurses will make their work easier.

Homemade Stars

If there isn't a star within your sky,
    Pretend it's there!
Why, a make-believe one, swung wide and high,
    Is just as fair!
If you put it where you'll see it every night,
Just where the sky's particularly bright,
Your star is sure to guide your steps aright.

If there isn't any sunshine in your day,
    Why put some in!
If you've never made your sun that way,
    Oh, do begin!
This sunshine-making's hard, but you won't mind;
Keep on, and when it's done you're apt to find
The home-made brand's the very nicest kind!

— Author unknown

Fourth Speaker:

A small girl looking out the windows on a bitterly cold night was admonished by her mother, "Close the drapes and come close to the fire."

"Oh, no, Mother, I am enjoying looking out at the beautiful snow, you miss so much just sitting by the fire."

You will see such a bright future and so much beauty if you look beyond the comforts and problems of this earth to the beauties and glories of heaven, the place God prepared for his own. You may be unable to walk to the windows of this building and look at the beauties of God's world but rest assured He is preparing a world much more beautiful.

Read your Bible each day to keep before you the promises of the Father. If you have a friend here who cannot see well enough to read, read to him also.

Hymn: "On Jordan's Stormy Banks"

Leader:

We will close with prayer.

Our Father we would ask Thee to comfort and sustain each person here today. Help them to know You are the friend ever present with them. Give each a joyous faith and when life's day here is ended, may they have the peace of rest, we ask in the name of Christ our Saviour, Amen.

21. Practical Evangelism

Hymns:

"Bring Them In"
"Work for the Night Is Coming"
"Like A Mighty Army"
"Send the Light"

Scripture: Acts 1:8

Leader:

The church is engaged in a mighty warfare against the forces of evil in this world. The question we face is, How may we best face this battle in our own community? Before there can be a great ingathering of people there must be much planning and work. Our first speaker will tell us how we might start our strategy.

First Speaker:

Very few generals would go out to fight a battle until they had sent scouts ahead to spy out the camp of the enemy. As members of a church wishing to evangelize the lost in our community, we too must spy out the land. In order to do this effectively I would suggest a house to house census.

We could secure cards and meet some Sunday afternoon for the purpose of going out and finding the prospects. We might even bring a sack lunch and as soon as our morning services are over take one or two block assignments and go out to find the names and addresses of the lost and unenlisted people.

Leader:

That is an excellent idea, but after the people have been found what shall we do?

Second Speaker:

We should make at least two copies of each prospect card. One copy to be placed in a permanent file at the church and one to be given to the teacher of the class responsible for that age group.

Third Speaker:

Just giving the teacher a prospect card is not enough. I think the teacher should be required to visit or have a class member visit that prospect. We should have a meeting of all the teachers and workers at a set time, say about two weeks after the cards have been given out. At this meeting each one should be asked to report on the results of his visit.

Leader:

After this meeting, if the prospects have not started attending our church, what would you suggest?

Fourth Speaker:

I suggest that we keep cards in a permanent file and only remove them when they have joined or moved away. If the first visit did not bring results the teacher should try again. After the teacher has tried several times making a note of the visit on the card, a new visitor should be assigned to that prospect for a time. The visitors should seek to become friends with the prospect and unless the prospect asks them not to call again, they should keep trying.

Leader:

Do you think the Bible approves house to house visitation?

Fifth Speaker:

Acts 5:42 reads: "And daily in the temple, and in every house, they ceased not to teach and preach Jesus Christ."

Visitation really started in the New Testament. Jesus sent out workers in pairs.

Paul practiced the visitation method. In Acts 20:20 he states, "...but [I] have showed you, and have taught you publicly, and from house to house."

Visitation is the secret of the growth of the early Christian movement. It will mean the success of our churches in this present day.

Sixth Speaker:

Sometimes churches seem to grow self-satisfied and grow into something like exclusive clubs. One feels as they visit them that they are unwelcome. Luke 14:23 teaches, "Go out into the highways and hedges, and compel them to come in, that my house may be filled."

We have a duty to go and visit the lost and unenlisted.

Seventh Speaker:

I like to have something to leave when I visit. We should have a card with a picture of our church, the time of services, our pastor's phone number, and a very special invitation for the person visited to attend. The visitor should write his own name on the card also.

Leader:

As we close I want to ask the question so often sung in the years gone by.

> Must I go, and empty-handed,
> Thus my dear Redeemer meet?
> Not one day of service give Him,
> Lay no trophy at His feet?
> Must I go, and empty-handed?
> Must I meet my Saviour so?
> Not one soul with which to greet Him:
> Must I empty-handed go?
> — George Stebbins

(Closing prayer)

We cannot recall the years we have wasted. Forgive us our neglect. Help us to fill our hands in the future with souls won for the Master, in His name we pray. Amen.

22. Youth Night Service

This program is designed to use all the members of a youth group in a church. It is suitable for a night when the pastor needs a supply or a special service.

The young people should be seated across the stage or in the choir. If your church approves of musical instruments in the services, those with instruments should sit in a group at one side.

Leader:

We have titled our program, *Consecration.* The word *consecration* comes from a Hebrew word *Kadesh,* meaning "to be holy," often rendered *sanctify,* or *dedicate.* We are young but we are dedicated to serve our Lord.

Music Director sings, "It Is No Secret" *(Young people hum until last phrase, then all join in.)*

First Speaker:

(Walks to center stage.) It is no secret to my friends and neighbors what God has done for me. *(Gives personal testimony.)*

(Leader reads John 3:3, 7.)

Youth group: "All Because of Calvary." (Many of the songs litsed can be found in *Youth Sings.*

Second Speaker:

It is because of Calvary I have consecrated my life to serve the Lord.

> Oh, the hush'd and holy quiet
> That Jehovah will impart,
> When He comes to make His dwelling
> In the consecrated heart!
>
> Oh, the hush and holy quiet!
> Oh, the rest while here below!

When He comes and fills His temple,
    Waves of glory o'er thee flow.

Blest the thought that our Jehovah
    Deigns to dwell in hearts so low!
And His presence gives this quiet,
    Which the world cannot bestow.

What a rest and what a stillness,
    Though without the winds may blow!
If Jehovah keeps His temple,
    Naught but rest the heart can know.
                              — John Newkirk

Duet: "Follow, I Will Follow Thee" *(Youth Sings,* page 25,) or *Youth Group:* "To God Be the Glory"

Third Speaker:

See that ye refuse not Him that speaketh (Hebrews 12:25).

Fourth and Fifth Speakers (in unison):

But as he which hath called you is holy, so be ye holy in all manner of conversation; because it is written, Be ye holy; for I am holy (I Peter 1:15, 16).

Solo: "How Great Thou Art"

(Sixth Speaker gives personal testimony)

Youth Group: "Battle Hymn of the Republic"
(If possible have two or three trumpets come in on the high notes.)

Leader:

Let us bow our heads for a prayer of consecration.

                My body, soul and spirit,
                    Jesus I give to Thee,
                A consecrated offering,
                    Thine evermore to be.

                My all is on the altar,
                    I'm waiting for the fire;
                Waiting, waiting, waiting,
                    I'm waiting for the fire.
                              — Unknown

(As the leader reads the closing prayer let the group repeat in unison after each line of the last verse:

1. All on the altar, Lord.
2. We wait for the fire,
3. Waiting, waiting, waiting.
4. We wait for the fire.)

23. We Are Thankful

Hymn: "Count Your Blessings"

Scripture: (Use two readers, one on each side of the stage.):

First Reader:

Stand thou still awhile that I may shew thee the Word of God (I Samuel 9:27).

Second Reader:

Consider how great things he hath done for you (I Samuel 12:24).

First Reader:

Are the consolations of God small with thee? (Job 15:11).

Second Reader:

When He giveth quietness, who then can make trouble? (Job 24:29).

First Reader:

The Lord shall give thee rest from thy sorrow and from thy fear (Isaiah 14:3).

Second Reader:

There hath not failed one word of all his good promises (I Kings 8:56).

Leader:

There are 31,000 promises in the Bible. They mean just what they promise. We fail so often to receive these blessings because we fail to ask for them.

We have so many things for which to be thankful it is our plan tonight to bring to mind just a few.

Music director leads all the youth on the stage in singing, "Thank You, Lord, for Saving My Soul." *(Youth Sings,* page 100.)

First Speaker:

My greatest blessing. May I tell you about the greatest thing that ever happened to me? (Tells of time when Christ came into his heart.)

First Reader (still in place at side of stage):

"All have sinned and came short of the glory of God" (Romans 3:23).

Second Reader:

And him that cometh to me I will in no wise cast out (John 6:37b).

Youth Group: "What a Friend We Have in Jesus."

Second Speaker:

The blessings of friendship. Of course I consider my greatest friend, my Saviour and the Lord. I find comfort and joy in talking to Him throughout the day. I also count it a great blessing to have Christian friends here on earth — friends who believe in me when at time I doubt myself; friends who will accept me as I am and not constantly be trying to find fault.

I enjoy friends my own age, they help me to keep abreast in school and in social life. I am thankful for my older friends — my teachers, pastor, and parents who have traveled life's road before me and want only to guide me away from the pitfalls. I hope when I am older I will remember the help I received when young and be a friend to a boy or girl.

First Reader:

A friend loveth at all times (Proverbs 17:17).

Second Reader:

A man that hath friends must shew himself friendly; and there is a friend that sticketh closer than a brother (Proverbs 18:24).

Solo, Duet, or Youth Group: "Why Do I Sing about Jesus?"

Third Speaker: Work is a blessing.

(Gives brief testimony about what it means for youth to work, then reads the following poem):

Work

Thank God for the might of it —
The ardor, the urge, the delight of it.
Work that springs from the heart's desire,
Setting the brain and soul on fire.
Oh, what is so good as the heat of it,
And what is so good as the beat of it?
And what is so kind as the stern command,
Challenging brain, and heart, and hand?
Work the Titan, work the Friend,
Shaping the earth to a glorious end,
Draining the swamps and blasting the hills,
Doing whatever the Spirit wills —
Rending the continent apart
To answer the dream of the master heart.
Thank God for a world where none may shirk;
Thank God for the splendor of work!

           — Morgan

Leader:

We are thankful for: *(young people stand one by one and say one or two words such as:* our parents, our church, our friends, our homes, our teachers, our pastor, our country, our freedom of speech. *Use as many words as you have people on the stage. Pass the words out ahead of time so there will be no hesitating.)*

Youth Group: "We Thank Thee, O God." (Written by B. D. Ackley.)

Leader:

For our closing prayer will all of you repeat with me Psalm 103:1, 2?

"Bless the Lord, O my soul: and all that is within me, bless his holy name. Bless the Lord, O my soul, and forget not all his benefits."